Time to Sign with Music
Preschooler-School Age

1. Breakfast, Lunch & Dinner 2
2. Color Song 4
3. Hands Can Count 8
4. It's Summer Time Again 10
5. I've Been Workin' on the Railroad 16
6. London Bridge 18
7. Mulberry Bush......................... 22
8. Over the River and Through the Woods 26
9. School Bus 30
10. Shape Song 34
11. She'll Be Coming Around the Mountain....... 38
12. Snack Song 46
13. Tell Me Why 50
14. The Ants Go Marching In 52
15. The Bear Went Over the Mountain 54
16. The More We Sign Together............... 56
17. The Transportation Song 58
18. Traffic Light 62
19. Use Your Manners...................... 64
20. What Will the Weather Be? 68

"Breakfast, Lunch and Dinner"
(Copyright©2003 Time to Sign, Inc.)

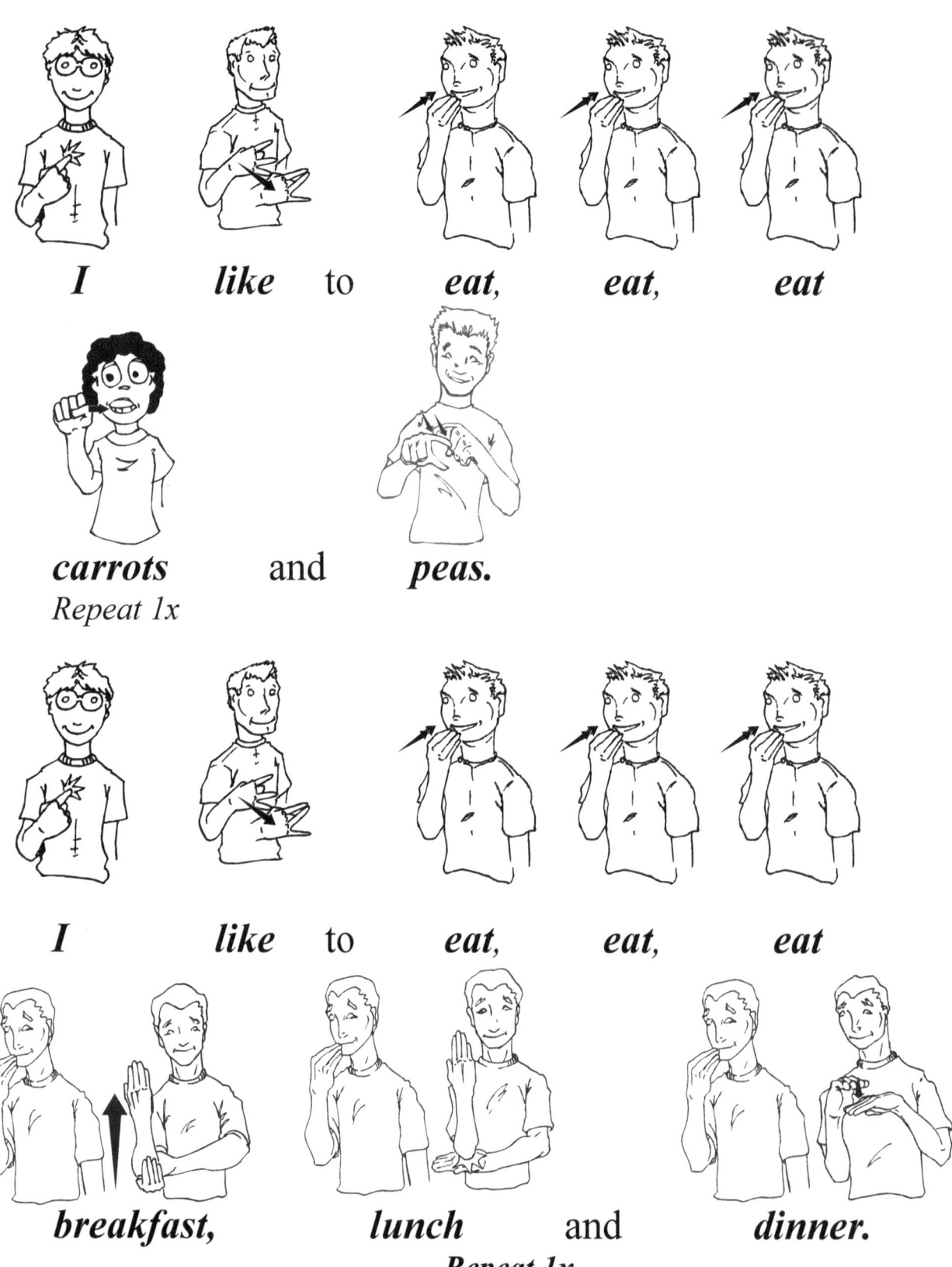

"Color Song"

(Copyright©2003 Time to Sign, Inc., Tune of Wheels on the Bus)

The **colors** of the **grass** are **green** and **brown**, **green** and **brown**, **green** and **brown**.
The **colors** of the **grass** are **green** and **brown**.

all   **around**   the   **world.**

The **colors** of **apples** are **red**, or **green**, **red** or **green**, **red** or **green**.
The **colors** of **apples** are **red**, or **green**,

The *colors* of the *sky* are *blue* and *white,*
blue and *white, blue* and *white.*
The *colors* of the *sky* are *blue* and *white.*

The *colors* of the *sun* are *yellow* and *gold,*
yellow and *gold, yellow* and *gold*
The *colors* of the *sun* are *yellow* and *gold.*

all *around* the *world.*

The *colors* of *pumpkins* are *orange* and *green,*
orange and *green,* *orange* and *green.*
The *colors* of *pumpkins* are *orange* and *green.*

all *around* *the* *world.*

The *colors* of *flowers* are *purple* and *pink,*
purple and *pink,* *purple* and *pink.*
The *colors* of *flowers* are *purple* and *pink.*

all   *around*   the   *world.*

The *colors* of the *night* are *black* and *white*, *black* and *white*, *black* and *white*.
The *colors* of the *night* are *black* and *white*,

all   *around*   the   *world.*

"Hands Can Count"
(Copyright©2002 Time to Sign, Inc.)

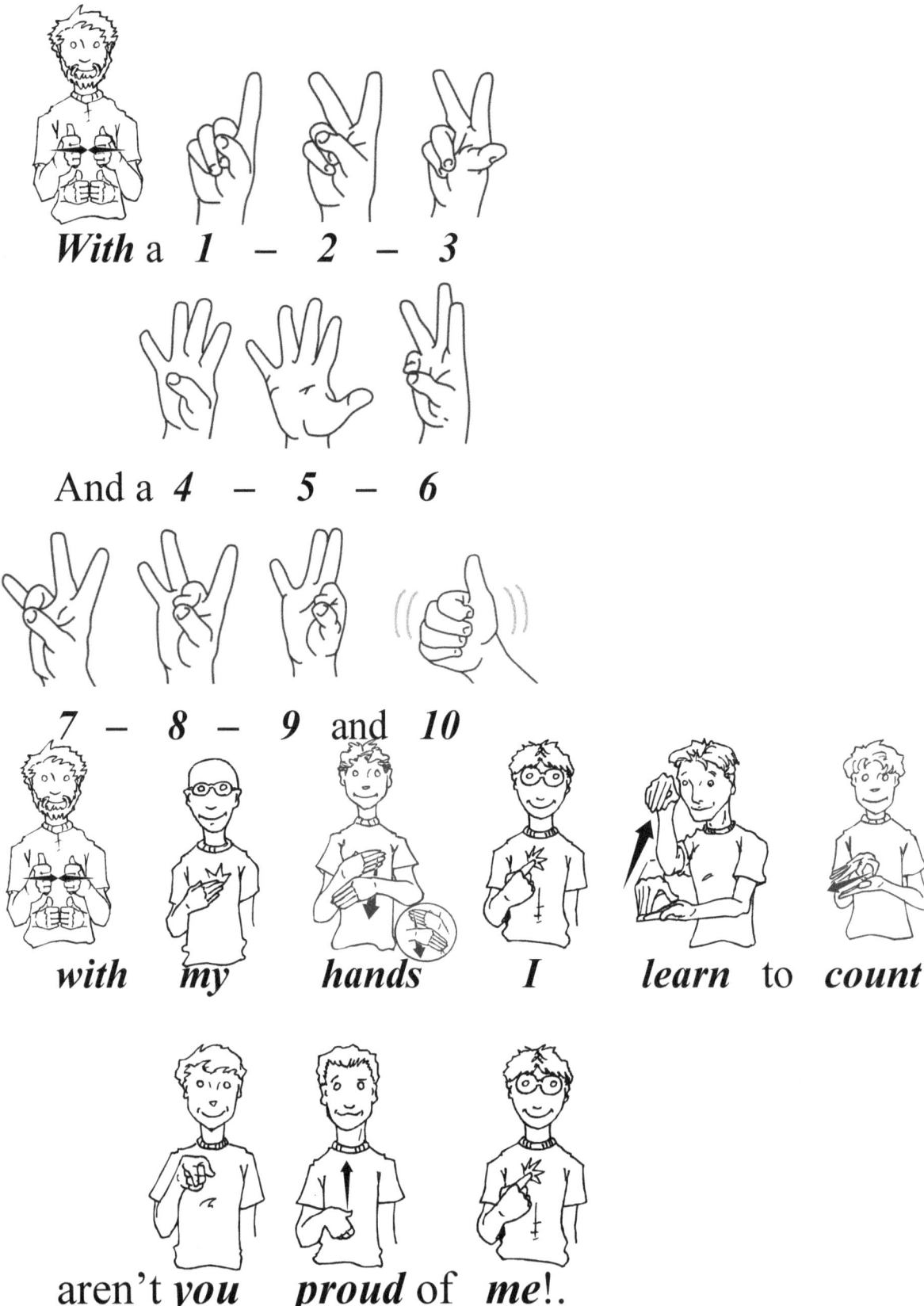

"It's Summer Time Again"
(Copyright©2003 Time to Sign, Inc., Tune of "The Farmer in the Dell")

what a *time* *we* will *have*

we'll *all* *go* to the *beach*.

We'll *all* *go* out and *camp,* (Repeat 1x)

what a *time* *we* will *have*

"I've Been Workin' on the Railroad"
(Original Author Unknown, Illustrations Copyright©2003 Time to Sign, Inc.)

I've been *workin'* on the *railroad*

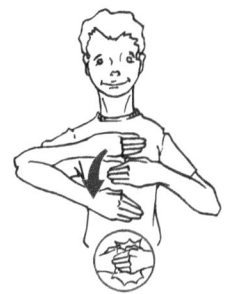 

all the live long *day.*

I've been *workin'* on th *railroad*

just to *pass* the *time* *away*.

"London Bridge"
(Traditional, Illustrations Copyright©2003 Time to Sign, Inc.)

London   bridge is *falling down, falling down, falling down.*

London   bridge is *falling down*

my   fair   lady.

Build it up ***with   iron   bars,***

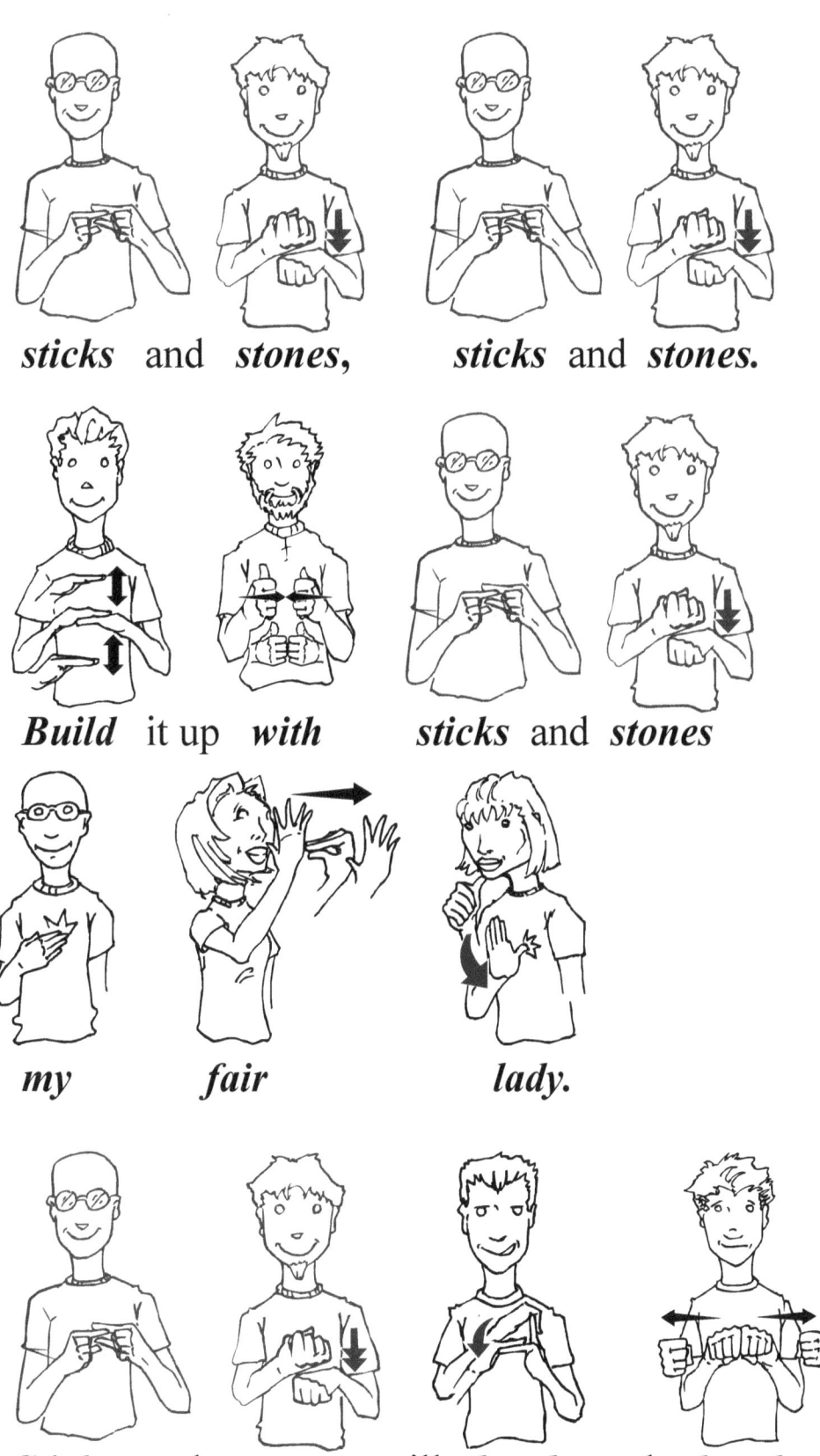

bend and *break,* *bend* and *break.*

Sticks and *stones* will *bend* and *break*

my *fair* *lady.*

"Mulberry Bush"
(Traditional, Illustrations Copyright©2003 Time to Sing, Inc.)

so *early* in the *morning.*

This is the *way*   *we* *comb* our *hair*, *comb* our *hair*, *comb* our *hair.*

This is the *way*   *we* *comb* our *hair*, so *early* in the *morning.*

This is the *way*   *we* *brush* our *teeth*, *brush* our *teeth,*

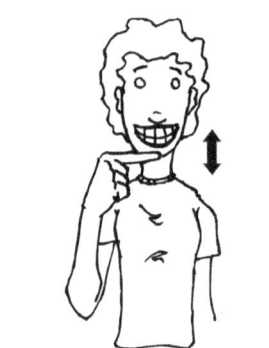

brush our *teeth.*

This is the *way*   we   *brush* our *teeth*

so *early*   in the   *morning.*

"Over the River and Through the Woods"
(Traditional, Illustrations Copyright©2003 Time to Sign, Inc.)

and drifting *snow.*

Over   the   ***river***   and   ***through***   the   ***woods***

oh   how   the   ***wind***   does   ***blow***!

   *(Point to toes)*      *(Point to nose)*

It   ***stings***   the   **toes**   and   ***bites***   the   **nose**

As *over* the *fields* *we* *go.*

"School Bus"

(Copyright©2002 Time to Sign, Inc., Tune of "The Farmer in the Dell")

The *school* bus *comes* for *me.*
The *school bus comes* for *me.*

Hey, ho, its *time* to *go*

The *school* *bus* *comes* for *me.*

First   we   ***pick up*** (use letter of name or sign name).

Next   we   ***pick up*** (use letter of name or sign name).

Then   we   ***pick up*** (use letter of name or sign name).

Last   we   ***pick up*** (use letter of name or sign name).

Now we're all at school.

Now we're all at school.

Clap

Clap and *cheer* we're finally *here.*

Now we're all at school.

"Shape Song"
(Copyright©2003 Time to Sign, Inc., Tune of Wheels on the Bus)

The *shape* of the *ball* is   *round*,   *round*,   *round*,
round, *round*, *round*,   *round*, *round*, *round*.
The *shape* of the *ball* is *round*, *round*, *round*

all   *around*   the   *school.*

The *shape* of the *blocks* are *square*, *square*, *square*,
square, *square*, *square*,   *square*, *square*, *square*.
The *shape* of the *blocks* are *square*, *square*, *square*

all *around* the *school.*

The *shape* of a *desk* is *rectangle*, *rectangle*, *rectangle*. The *shape* of a *desk is rectangle*

all *around* the *school.*

The *shape* of a *football* is *oval*, *oval*, *oval*.
The *shape* of a *football* is *oval*

all *around* the *school.*

The *shape* of the *roof* is a *triangle, triangle, triangle.*
The *shape* of the *roof* is a *triangle*

all *around* the *school.*

The *shape* of the *ball field* is a *diamond*, is a *diamond,* is a *diamond.*
The *shape* of a *ball field* is a *diamond*

all *around* the *school.*

The *shape* of a *valentine* is a *heart,*
is a *heart,* is a *heart.*
The *shape* of a *valentine* is a *heart*

all *around* the *school.*

"She'll be Coming Around the Mountain"
(Traditional, Illustrations Copyright©2003 Time to Sign, Inc.)

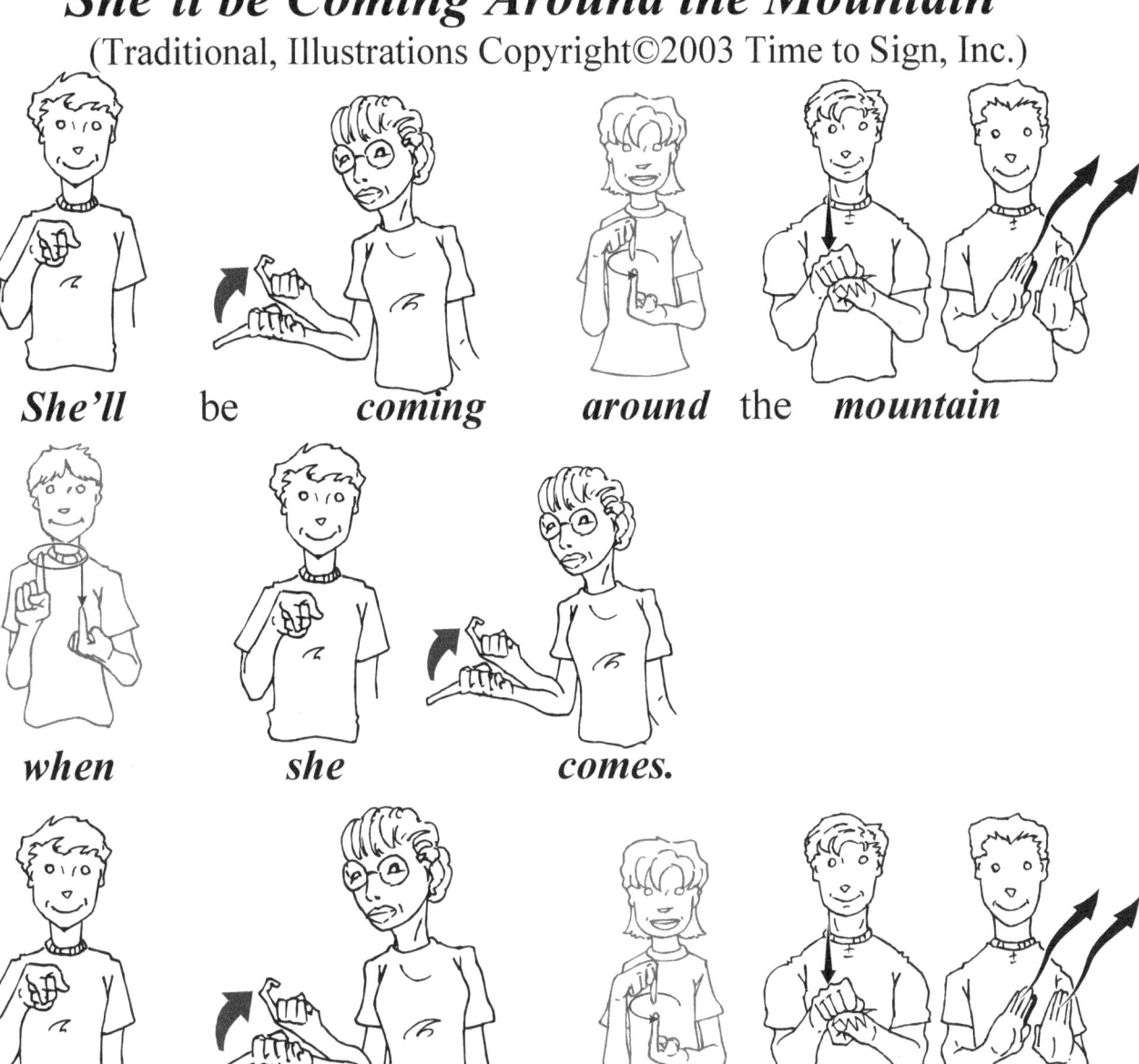

when *she* *comes.*

She'll be *coming* *around* the *mountain*
Repeat 2x

when *she* *comes.*

She'll be *riding* *six* *white* *horses*

(Shout Hee Haw)

when *she* *comes.*

Oh, *we* will all *go* out to *meet* *her*

when *she* *comes.*

Oh, *we* will all *go* out to *meet* *her*
Repeat 2x

when *she* *comes.*

"Snack Song"
(Copyright Time to Sign, Inc. 2002, tune of Row, Row, Row Your Boat)

Happily, happily, happily, happily, I clean-up and play.

"Tell Me Why"
(Traditional, Illustrations Copyright©2002 Time to Sign, Inc.)

And *I* will *tell* *you* *why* *I* *love* *you.*

"The Ants Go Marching In"

(Original Author Unknown, Illustrations Copyright©2002 Time to Sign, Inc.)

ants

marching

ground

The ants go marching one by one, hurrah, hurrah
The ants go marching one by one, hurrah, hurrah
The ants go marching one by one,
The little one stops to suck his thumb
And they all go marching down to the ground
To get out of the rain, BOOM! BOOM! BOOM!...

shoe

The ants go marching two by two, hurrah, hurrah
The ants go marching two by two, hurrah, hurrah
The ants go marching two by two,
The little one stops to tie his shoe
And they all go marching down to the ground
To get out of the rain, BOOM! BOOM! BOOM!...

tree

The ants go marching three by three, hurrah, hurrah
The ants go marching three by three, hurrah, hurrah
The ants go marching three by three,
The little one stops to climb a tree
And they all go marching down to the ground
To get out of the rain, BOOM! BOOM! BOOM!...

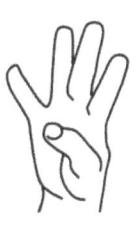 

door

The ants go marching four by four, hurrah, hurrah
The ants go marching four by four, hurrah, hurrah
The ants go marching four by four,
The little one stops to shut the door
And they all go marching down to the ground
To get out of the rain, BOOM! BOOM! BOOM!...

dive

The ants go marching five by five, hurrah, hurrah
The ants go marching five by five, hurrah, hurrah
The ants go marching five by five,
The little one stops to take a dive
And they all go marching down to the ground
To get out of the rain, BOOM! BOOM! BOOM!...

The ants go marching six by six, hurrah, hurrah
The ants go marching six by six, hurrah, hurrah
The ants go marching six by six,
The little one stops to pick up sticks
And they all go marching down to the ground
To get out of the rain, BOOM! BOOM! BOOM!...

 sticks

The ants go marching seven by seven, hurrah, hurrah
The ants go marching seven by seven, hurrah, hurrah
The ants go marching seven by seven,
The little one stops to pray to heaven
And they all go marching down to the ground
To get out of the rain, BOOM! BOOM! BOOM!...

 pray

The ants go marching eight by eight, hurrah, hurrah
The ants go marching eight by eight, hurrah, hurrah
The ants go marching eight by eight,
The little one stops to shut the gate
And they all go marching down to the ground
To get out of the rain, BOOM! BOOM! BOOM!...

  gate

The ants go marching nine by nine, hurrah, hurrah
The ants go marching nine by nine, hurrah, hurrah
The ants go marching nine by nine,
The little one stops to check the time
And they all go marching down to the ground
To get out of the rain, BOOM! BOOM! BOOM!...

  time

The ants go marching ten by ten, hurrah, hurrah
The ants go marching ten by ten, hurrah, hurrah
The ants go marching ten by ten,
The little one stops to say "THE END"
And they all go marching down to the ground
To get out of the rain, BOOM! BOOM! BOOM!...

 THE END

rain

hurrah

stop

"The Bear Went Over the Mountain"
(Traditional, Illustrations Copyright©2003 Time to Sign, Inc.)

The **bear** went **over** the **mountain**
Repeat 2x

to **see** **what** **he** **could** **see.**
Repeat 2x

The **other** **side** of the **mountain**
Repeat 2x

that's *all* that *he* *could* *see.*

"The More We Sign Together"
(Traditional, Illustrations Copyright©2002 Time to Sign, Inc.)

The *more* we *sign* *together*, *together*, *together*,

The *more* we *sign* *together*, the *happier we'll* *be*.

'Cause *your* *friends* are *my* *friends*,

And *my* *friends* are *your* *friends*.

The *more* *we* *sign* *together* the *happier we'll* *be*.

"The Transportation Song"
(Copyright©2002 Time to Sign, Inc., Tune of "She'll be Coming Around the Mountain")

We will *sail* on the *ocean* in a *ship*.
Repeat 1x

We will *sail* on the *ocean*.
Repeat 1x

We will *sail* on the *ocean* in a *ship*.

We will **ride** on the **rails** in a **train**.
Repeat 1x

We will **ride** on the **rails**.
Repeat 1x

We will **ride** on the **rails** in a **train**.

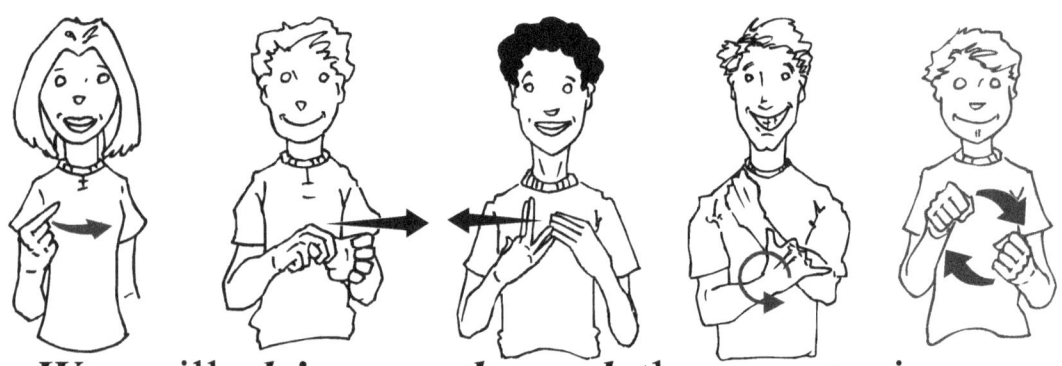

We will **drive** **through** the **country** in a **car**.
Repeat 1x

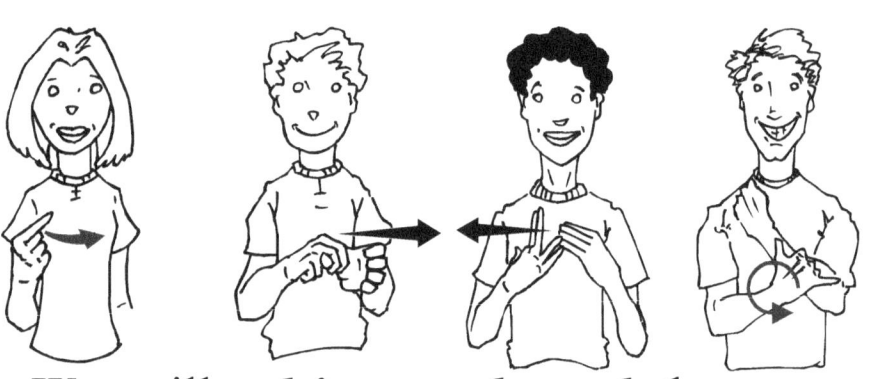

We will **drive** **through** the **country.**
Repeat 1x

We will **drive** **through** the **country** in a **car**.

"Traffic Light"//
(Traditional - Tune of "Mary Had A Little Lamb", Illustrations Copyright©2003 Time to Sign, Inc.)

Can **you** **see** the ***traffic light***,

the ***traffic light***, the ***traffic light***?

Green means ***go*** and ***yellow*** means ***slow***,

and *red* means *STOP, STOP, STOP!*
Repeat song

"Use Your Manners"
(Copyright©2002 Time to Sign, Inc.)

Use **your** **manners** in **your** **home**

or **when** **you** **play**.

Use **your** **manners** **with** **your** **friends**,

Use them *today*.

Like *saying* "*Please*" and "*Thank You*" to those *around*.

It's a whole lot *better* than *being* a *clown*.

Make your *friends* *feel* **special** in what *you* **say**.

Using **manners** is the ***only way***.

Use *your* *manners* in *your* *home*

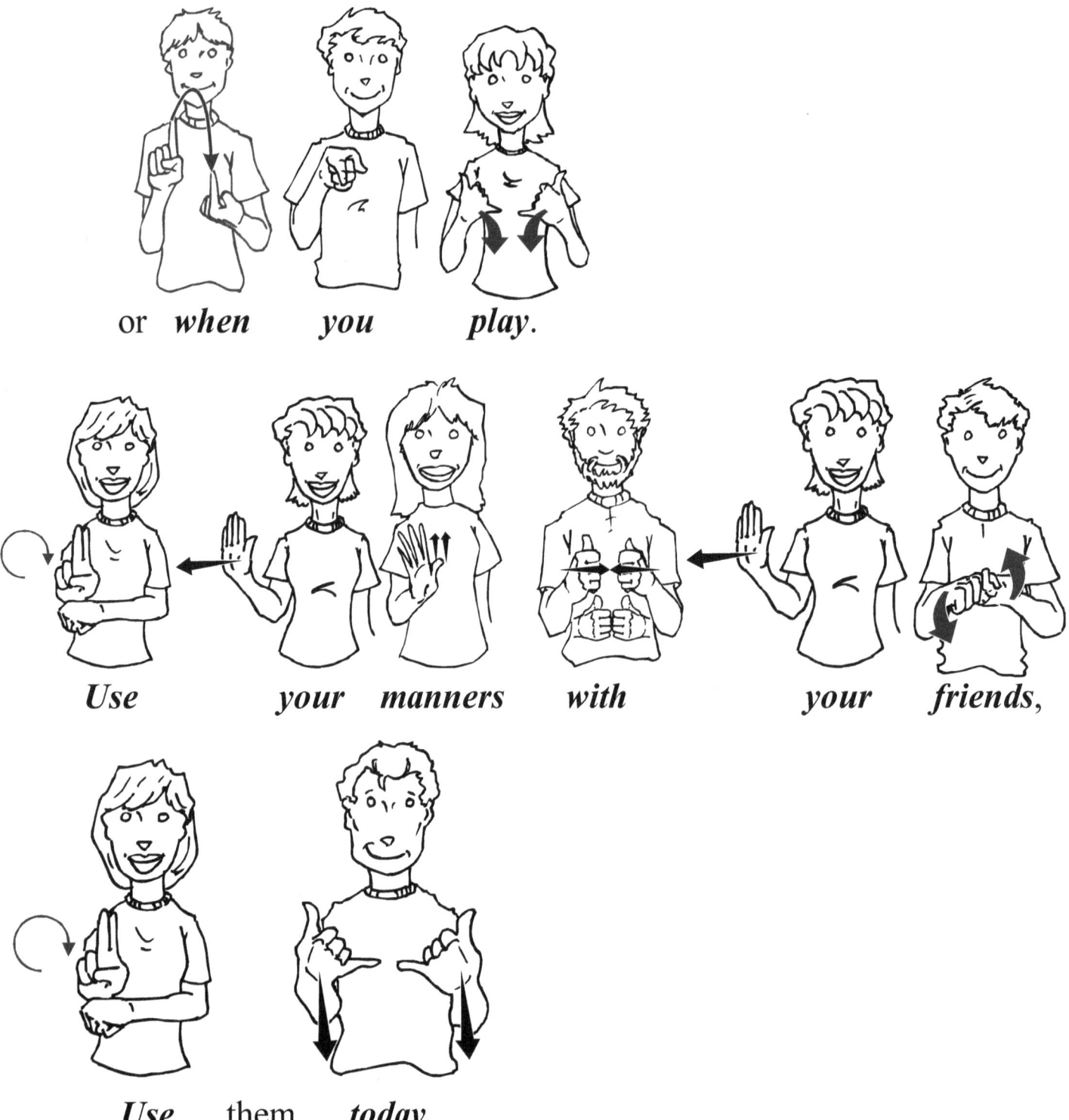

"What Will The Weather Be?"

(Original Author Unknown - Tune of What Will the Matter Be?, Illustrations Copyright©2002 Time to Sign, Inc.)

Oh dear, *what* will the *weather* *be*?

Oh dear, *what* will the *weather* *be*?

Sunny, **rainy**, **windy**, or **snowy**,

what will the *weather* *be*?

Time to Sign with Music
Preschool/School Age
Free CD with all accompanying music available
by contacting contact@timetosign.com

Time to Sign with Music Infant/Toddler Book and CD
16 Songs to Sign

- Animals on the Farm
- Apples and Bananas
- Bumble Bee
- Five Little Monkeys
- Happy Little Child
- If You're Happy and You Know It
- Itsy-Bitsy Spider
- Muffin Man
- Please and Thank You
- Row, Row Your Boat
- Six Little Ducks
- Ten Little Indians
- Three Little Monkeys
- Twinkle Little Star
- Where Are My Pets?
- Where is Thumbkin?

Time to Sign with Music Toddler/Preschool Book and CD
18 Songs to Sign

- ABC's (slow version)
- ABC's
- Bingo
- Buckle Bear Safety Song
- Car Song
- Down By the Station
- Fruit Song
- I'm a Firefighter
- I'm a Police Officer
- Make New Friends
- Mr. Sun
- Old McDonald Had A Farm
- Seven Days
- The Five Senses Song
- Veggies Song

Copyright©2003-2014 Time to Sign, Inc.

Great Resources Available at
www.timetosign.com

To order additional Time to Sign products please visit our web-site
www.TimeToSign.com or call (321) 726-9466

MICHAEL & LILLIAN HUBLER

ABOUT THE AUTHORS

Michael and Lillian Hubler founded Time to Sign, Inc. in 2000. The company was founded because the Hublers' recognized the benefits of using American Sign Language (ASL) with their own children, as well as with other children, families, educators, and care givers around the world. Time to Sign programs have been used in Family Childcares, Private Preschools, Early Head Start, Head Start, and School Districts.

Lillian is a nationally acclaimed presenter/trainer. Since 2000, she has trained over 50,000 educators, parents and children around the world in age appropriate and developmentally appropriate sign language usage. She is renowned for her high energy workshops and presentations. She has appeared on CNN, ABC, NBC, and has been interviewed by Florida Today and the Washington Post.

Michael is Director of Educational Curriculum and Product Development for Time to Sign. He is currently working on his doctoral dissertation in the field of education, specializing in the positive impacts of sign language on social and emotional development. Michael has served as an executive director for various educational and community services organizations, specializing in services and programs to enhance the education, personal growth, and development of at-risk children.

Michael and Lillian also owned a licensed day care with 135 children from birth to 12 years of age. They have written over 25 sign language books, including preschool and school-age curriculums. Time to Sign's trainings and materials are uniquely designed to promote social-emotional development and reduce children's challenging behavior in social settings. Their training programs and materials also promote literacy, language development, and communication.